Get Out The Kitchen Grace

By Kimberly and Grace-Marie Housley

Grace-Marie,

Thank you for waking me up to life.

-Mom

Grace...Get out the kitchen!

Oh no Grace, not the eggs.

Grace...Get out the kitchen!

Oh no Grace, that is not his food.

Grace...Get out the kitchen!

Oh no Grace, that's my brand new seasoning.

Grace...Get out the kitchen!

Oh no Grace, is that my popcorn?

Grace...Get out the kitchen!

Oh no Grace, not all the
bananas?

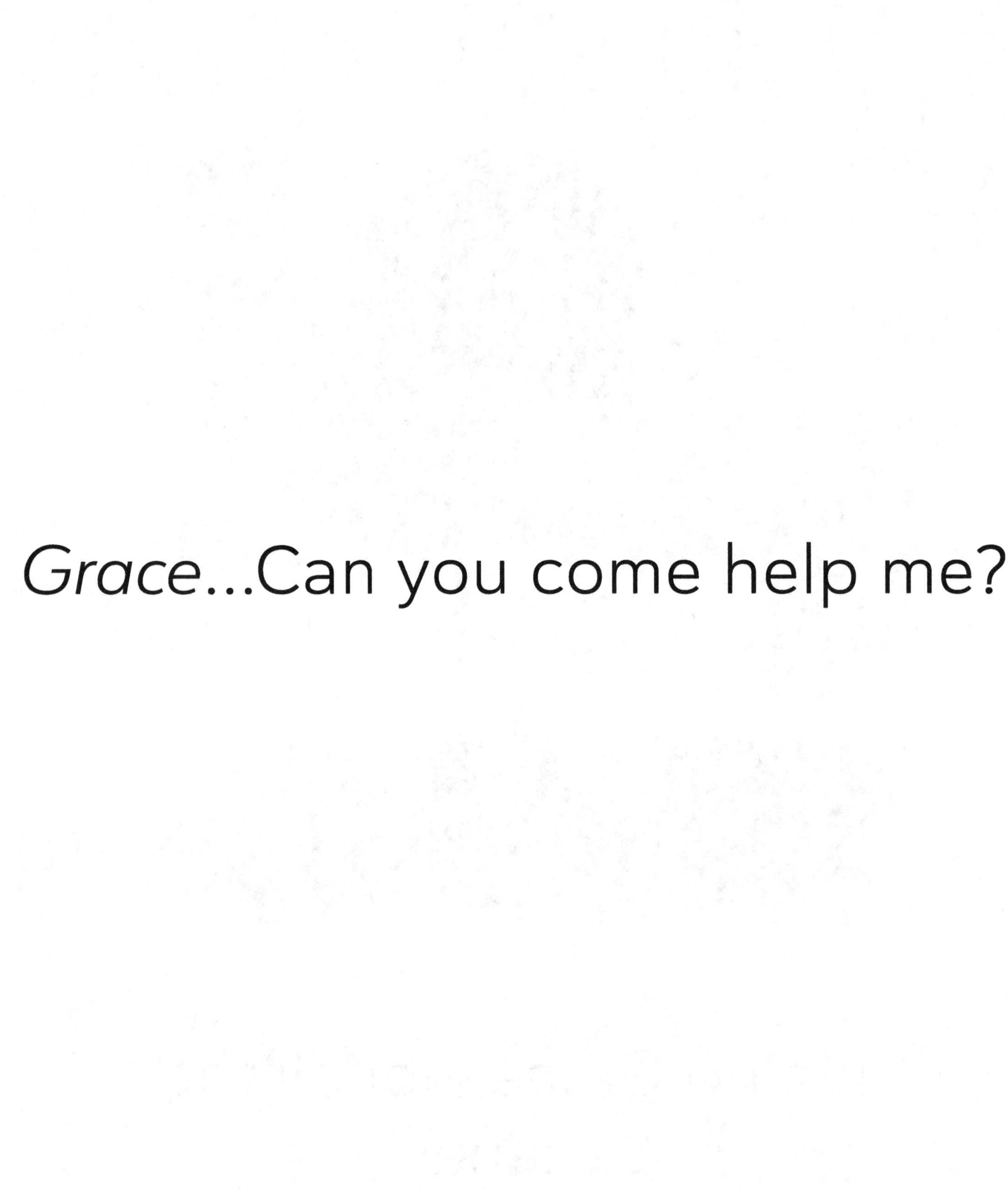

Grace...Can you come help me?

My Grace, you love the kitchen.